DISCOUNTED

poems by Misti Rainwater-Lites

© Paroxysm Press 2018.

No part of this publication may be reproduced or transmitted in any form without the written permission of the publisher - apart from limited reproduction for the purposes of review, criticism or research as allowed under the Copyright Act 1968.

Paroxysm Press
PO Box 3107
Rundle Mall
Adelaide
5000
[Australia]

www.paroxysmpress.com
www.facebook.com/paroxysmpress
www.twitter.com/paroxysmpress
www.instagram.com/paroxysmpress

DISCOUNTED
Misti Rainwater-Lites
ISBN 978-1-876502-20-1

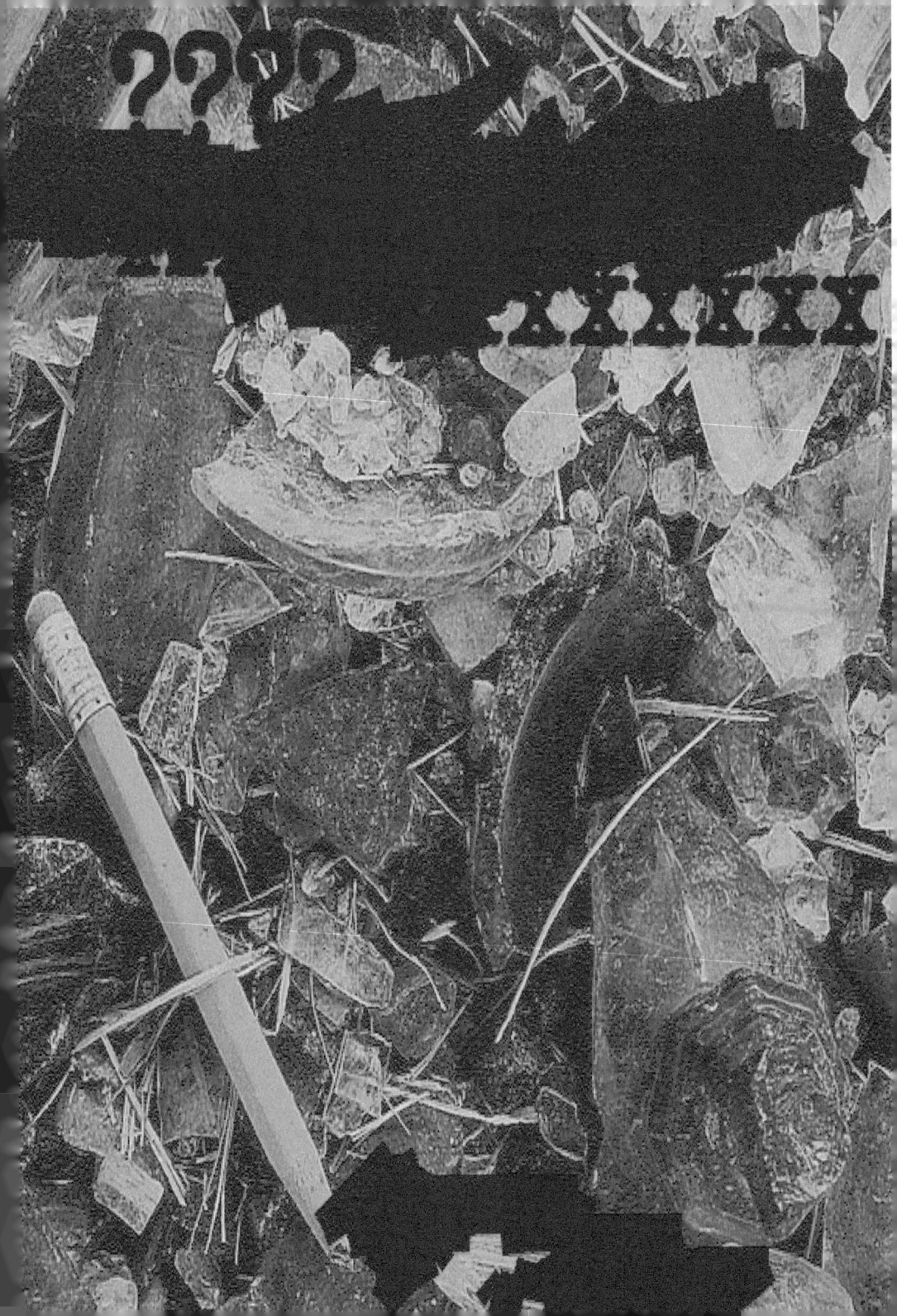

Xmas Ball

All I want, finally, is one magical dress
stiffer and stronger
than angel wings
to carry me cherished
across the sea.
That's a fucking laugh.
I bleed red and green neon script,
a kind of invitation.
Men notice these things,
smell these wounds with
their wild coyote noses.
I'm dirty cum rag,
jerk off whore,
Texas trash
crumpled into a ball
thrown with remarkable aim
into the receptacle
that is
never full.

Blue Moon

I'm sitting on the bed I share
with my ex-husband
crying because I am stuck
and too weak to be stoic.
The ex is in the den
with his soul mate, the television.
Our son asks me why I am crying
then says,"Stop that crying
or I'll give you something to cry about!"
I laugh through the blood
of my broken fucking heart.
It's science.
It's an art, this sangre de HA HA business.
I put on my clown face
my bleak whore mask
my screaming colors
and wade through it
with my cowboy boots on.
The ex enters the room, tells our son,
"Mommy wants to fly to many different places."
I'm stinking up the cage.
The door will open and I will go,
leaving a little boy
with feathers and blood.
I hope he will make
good use
of the
quill.

King Shit Kicker

Mother's rot feeds the roses.
Meanwhile Daddy looms all
over the house.
Even the attic bulges.
The basement is Fuck Central.
The faces blur while one voice
sticks crooked in my ear.
You can guess whose.
There is nothing so romantic
as a North Texas drawl
dripping Baptist guilt
all over orgasm flushed tits.
There is nothing at all frantic
about this feverish process.
Fuck me like I'm already gone.
Fuck me into the future
where I am buried
and my smug replacement
models dresses for you
the color of sno cones.
She will be the right kind of girl,
the kind who comes
from a vacant house
everything tidy
and cordial
in its corner.

SLURP

I think God is schizophrenic.
He keeps confusing my order.
I'm on the beach, salty, tossed from too many storms.
In other words, yes, I'm hurricane haunted mermaid bones.
I jangle so juicy when I walk.
But this road doesn't lead where it's supposed to.
How do I keep missing the sunrise on Key West?
Koko Loko and Kim Wu won't hold the table forever.
I think God is fucking with me.
In my sleep on the long way home I cry out for Mom
like she's the angel driving the van through clouds
like she knows the route
like she is magic enough to shake the seeds from my skull.
This communion is not what I was hoping for.
This bread doesn't come from the surest oven.
I don't know where you got these grapes, mister, but no way in hell
am I drinking this discounted wine.
There are other
tourists for that.
Easily tricked and led to the rocks
where everything breaks
to the manic delight
of the gossiping gulls.

Chatter

Even psycho cyber sluts need romance so lie, goddamn it.
Present the pretense of adoration.
Or don't.
Sometimes all a gal needs to make it through is,
"Check your inbox."

The poet/editor from Liverpool sends a new cock shot.
This is his cock looking surprised.
This is his cock freed from his "boxies."
This is his cock shooting its fuckload into a pair of your panties.
"You know I've been a fan of yours for years but right now I need to get off," he writes.

The sun sets all over the Mersey.
The sun spits viscera across the San Antonio sky.
Somebody somewhere loves someone so hard it hurts.
Meanwhile the rabbit vibrator needs new batteries.

After T. S. Eliot

There are no eyes here. There is no seeing.
There is plenty of believing.
Believe the blood.
Believe the bile.
Believe the cunt bitchery, the broken glass, the twisting knives.
Believe the bullets.
Believe the war.
Believe the grasping the snatching the grabbing hands.
There is feasting. Bounty of bones. Banquet of beg.
There is swill and there is gulp and there are cries for more.
Blind infant mewl blind toddler crawl blind beating of winged fists.
Black choked sky closed to smoke signals and shallow sacrifices.
You cannot see for all the ash.
There are miles of this.
The air is stoic with this.
This is a church but also a bakery.
All of us are risen.

DORME MECUM

It's fucking basic.
It's elementary.
You're long in tooth, doll.
You should get it by now.
When a man sends you a picture
of his cock it's not intellectual discourse
and emotional intimacy he's after.
There won't be an airport meeting.
Forget fucking on an actual train.
This is where trains and hotel rooms
are invisible and you cannot smell
the cum or piss or sweat or cologne.
Kisses are tasteless.
This works for most.
If it doesn't work for you
write a bitchy poem about it.
So used.
So discounted.
This is where the muse comes in
spreads her legs
and demands
a quick fuck
and a century of cuddle.
Blink.
Sneeze.
Pout.
It's over. It's dust.
The wicked world
continues.

Shameles. Quite.

She lures George Clooney to the alley behind the yogurt shop with her fierce fuck me eyes, drops to her knees, sucks him off, grabs Justin Bieber in front of the My Little Pony boutique, kisses him hard with George's cum fresh on her Botoxed pout, fondles Justin's ass until he begs her to stop with a breathless whine. Her dress is wrinkled but still shinier than a ripe Rome apple so she hails a taxi, takes it to the green side of town, fucks Ashton Kutcher saloon gal style on a table in the not-so-cool section. Ashton is loopy from the attention deficit disorder medication, cums inside her quivering pussy, pinwheels so gaga in his kicked puppy eyes. The day is still infantile so she hoofs it to La Cienega where all the hot shit motherfuckers congregate in the gourmet donut parking lot, kicks an aging and less than desirable Axl Rose in his balls because, bitch, he LIKES it like that, whispers,"I want to piss in your mouth" in his ear then disappears inside a maroon BMW with Jessica Simpson's new husband. "She's getting her nails done, love," he coos in her ear as she jacks him off to a Taylor Swift song.

Koko Loko Vents

aklfjasghah! ghahgiejgiei! hgahgierjeijgijieie!
AKDFHGIJEIJGIE!!!!@#$@$@$HGHGIEIFGHEIEIFGJEIGJkjdfgj!!
LLLLLLLLLLLLLLLLLLLLLLLLLLLLLLLLLLLLLLLLLLLLLLLLLLL
IIIIIIIIIIIIIIIIIIIIIIIIIIIIIIIIIIIIIIIIIIIIIIIIIIIIIIIIIIIIIIIIIIIIIII
KKKKKKKKKKKKKKKKKKKKKKKKKKKKKKKKKKKKKKKKKKKK
EEEEEEEEEEEEEEEEEEEEEEEEEEEEEEEEEEEEEEEEEEEEE
ajfkajf!r343jkja;jkfi48ijgkje;lkajlhgigjiaejf;akkdjf;alkjfkfj! DEMOCRAT REPUBLICAN WELFARE FOOD STAMP BUTT WASH!
eat burrito! eat shoe! food turn into doo doo in large intestine!
ANAL CANAL! Poop chute!
POKE POKE POKE POKE
POKE POKE POKE POKE
POKE POKE POKE me eyes out, mate!
poKepoKepoKepoKepoKepoKepoKepoKe...
wheeeeee!!!!!!!!!!!!!!!!!!
akfjdjfjdjdjdjdjdjghhghghiieixhxhihgieohgpahghiehgiahg!!!! ahgie!!! ahgiex!!!
garbage trucks starting up! sun spit viscera across bitch pleaSe sky!!!!
beer! whiskey! allergy pills! no sleep until Amarillo! motherFUCK!!$$$$$
dlskjfalkfjakdgjd!!! fakdjf;alsdfjdslkfj!!!! SEX! sock! package! SPECIAL DELIVERY!!!!!!!! SUCK PENIS! SWALLOW BABY BATTER, BITCH!!!!!!!!!
hyahgfueghgiehzhighephg xogho ghiejpghalseigp goehgiepglghoepepe

just called to say LOVE YOU just cozy in Cosby sweater just walking on sunshine just fucking around ye olde mulberry bush just humping

around like Bobby Brown on hot ass Saturday night in honky town
call me crazy call me not quite right call me substitute cheese ball
JUST CALL RIGHT NOW ON ROTARY PHONE alone bad place to be
when disco circus come to town other children so gay with balloons and confetti rockets lovers frolic to idiot choir song and la and la and
some kind of wOw !$%#%#%kjkakdjgijakjgoijlehalkgj; akdjakjkdkdkdkdk
put it in post
pubic hairs!!!!!!
non rhyme love poem truer than cheap motel soap!
cheese ass!
baby!
@RIGJGKFHGHJASKJKJLKSJDKDKDKDKDKDKD
(mayor of my marrow)
….ad nauseam…
this poem was found bloody and cruddy
beneath boardwalk
and also used condom
and soggy lipsticked cigarette

Who Will You Marry?

It's so accurate it's scary. He'll be made of steel he'll never cheat you he'll treasure your idiosyncrasies always with God on his tongue and his hands shiny with eBuLLieNCe juice. She'll be ultra lean and tragedy savvy your bell ringing Saturn angel/silver throat teacher glib but good through and through, training the horses in your corral to be bribed with rosiest apples and endless lumps of sugar. Ah the thrilling magic of us so cozy pearly in our shell, all alone in dark Ford with the city buzzing below and Buddy Holly on the radio promising us an amusement park flavored forever, fizzy with rainbow bubbles high above BURST.

Inspired By Chuck I'm American Goddamn It Norris

What I like about America. Wow. Well where does a girl begin? I am 39 but I live in America. I have lived with three different men. I have given birth twice. I have waited for emergency food stamps for five hours during a hurricane evacuation. I have road tripped with an anxious husband and babbling infant to Acuna, Mexico to load up on affordable medication. I have watched the cop car lights from the window of a crack whore shack in Nederland, Texas watching my paranoid schizophrenic brother being taken away because he assaulted my mother's third husband in my mother's third husband's own house. I don't miss my uterus. I don't miss all the blood. I am 39 but I live in America so I am still a girl. I'm so girlish giggling in line at the American cinema, high on Coca-Cola Classic and candy and hope. I'm such a girl treating myself to a pedicure at the strip mall after another nervous breakdown because the air-conditioner isn't working in the triple digit heat and the SUV has been towed and the mother is in town and bitching at me because I won't return the sister's phone calls and clean the son's room. There are so many toys. I don't know where to put them all.

What I like about America are the choices. Do I want cheese on my French fries? Sour cream? Bacon? Jalapenos? Smith and Wesson or Colt? Pawn shop or Walmart? Would I rather watch Kendra show her latest hot ass photographs to Hank or Kim run around Kourtney's mansion in a wig because she's soooo krazy? Which Teen Mom do I want to be when I grow up? Would I like the Facebook dick in my mouth or in my ass? Would I like to read my poems at the truck stop or Christ The Redeemer neon church across from the donut shop? Do I want the boy (Batman) or girl (My Little Pony) Happy Meal? Am I happy or eBuLLieNT? Misery is not a choice in America. Everyone is a cheerleader with perky tits and a bouncy ponytail.

How I spent my American summer vacation. Camp Fear. Camp Paranoia. Camp Virtual Sex. Camp Loathing. Camp Nausea. Camp Panic Attack. Camp Mediocre San Antonio Apartment Complex.

Where I hide and take pictures of dolls but do not grow older but remain a girl because I am an American cheeky and ridiculous in my blue and white gingham singing karaoke for my supper.

A Woman is a Kind of Wound

I was starving for meat but in the forest it all smells the same and I couldn't find my knives for all the cupcakes and angel skulls made of wax. A suffocation of mist then pomegranate Kool-Aid swallow and pregnancy vomit with a consternation of poker cards and no and never the ten of cups blazing rainbow joy and gleam grin peace but something else considerable dark iconoclast stoic all tricked out with sticking swords and mud vein pentacles a demonic smirk of coagulation. Commercials come candy consume conspire co-exist cherubic cluster captured caged clearly. . . kept.

Sodium

The baby wanted meatballs but there were no meatballs so
the mother fed him mini ravioli.
Jesus fucking CHRIST. 30% sodium.
There has to be a better way.

In the pool there were things floating around.
Dead things. Black specks. One green leaf, small and iridescent
in the bleaching sun. That was okay. The mother splashed water at the bee.
She knew the bee would not let it go. The bee would have its revenge.
The bee flew toward the mother's face. The mother held her nose with her fingers
and dipped down into the water. The chlorine stung her eyes.
The boy, not really a baby, stayed on the steps wearing his red plastic mask.
He was afraid of the water.

There are still pockets of surprise in America,
tiny sanctuaries untouched by free enterprise.
There are waterfalls. There are mesas. There is cool verdure.
You can still buy record albums
and Mexican comic books. Then there are the billboards advertising Jesus
and the seven pound burrito. There is escape, sure, but you have to
work like a motherfucker
to find it.

Dick Pictures

So much manic Crayola blur and then
straight to the inbox
concise cock
pink! thick! erection
perky prick
up to much good
silly with YUM.
Optimistic cocks are thumbs
sneering in mortality's granite maw.
Pink panties, soaked, silky smoking guns.
The cunt risks a blossom.
The curious nose loose in garden of happy accident.
If the accident will
slippery comfort
shadowed kinship
stranger creatures
poking around
electric lurk.

Candle

I was using a candle because he wasn't around.
39 is an itchy age.
You could say 39 is a waxy age.
Accuracy is a disintegrating commodity.
I keep
making wishes.

Christian Slater Plays God

On the score card of fuck he was aces, baby.
He looked like a less canny Christian Slater.
I crawled into his lap, camped out in his daddy bear recliner.
Our house was the color of lime flavored salt water taffy.
The space heater roared and we toasted with cups of blush.
The deer ran and the car swerved all over the back roads
and it was an after school special cautionary tale
starring Lucy from "Dallas" and Larry from "Three's Company."
Once there was fish but it rotted in the fridge.
Lots of other stuff was lost
and wasted.
There was a pawn shop in Vegas
a "Twilight Zone" episode now
never airs during the Fourth of July marathon
I'm the only one
who has seen it.

Oh Mister Hefner I Swear To Fucking GOD

You know what's weird, Hef?
It's a weird feeling
being a heterosexual woman
a mother, even
a sister, alas
a daughter, of course
masturbating to ancient Playboy pictorials
thinking The Women In These Pictures
Are Dead Now Or Well On Their Way.
That's pretty fucked up, you must admit.
I prefer the soft glossy airy lies, the bullshit fantasies
to the other stuff
but your fascination
with fake platinum fuck bots
is such a yawn
such a slap in the face
of true feminine beauty
which seems to elude
your pedestrian comprehension.
But I am broke and home on the sofa
each Saturday night
while you frolic and mingle
and chortle to camera flash
and grateful fondle.
I should like to wipe the sweat from your forehead.
I should like to kneel at your slippers
feel your gnarled hands in my hair
taste the mystical air that surrounds you
before I die
because I'm scared of leaving this plane
without your benediction
because you are all the God
I can stand.

Picnic on Saturn

The universe has prepared a picnic for us.
Don't come if you can't attend.
The alien ants have invaded my watermelon.
I'm not much without your consternation.
Too much Venus Neptune conjunction keeps me in nap mode.
We didn't come here to dream.
Your ice keeps me in business.
I'm solar exhibit number seven.
I've lost count
of all these suns.

FICTION

I'm stuck inside donut spins in a parking lot that isn't there anymore. It's a teenage car there's beer I'm twelve and my cousin is bleeding and my cousin has tits and the bridge is a yawn over snakes and mud. The town is the most real and continual fact of my life it is not a fiction it is not a memory I am living it still and I don't know what to call this other than rewind. The grandfather is alive and working the father is in another state the mother is decorating a house made of eyes and Cyndi Lauper provides candy scream and we are all trying too hard to prove our glee. I can't stop muttering FUCK YOU at the television. Something is wrong with the remote control.

I can't get out of this reality fast enough. It's late and presents are expected and I'm still stiff in petticoats but the air is thicker than blood and this tree is filled with skeletons and I don't know these bones and I won't name this horror because it is still happening and the eyes are watching and the mouths are filled with teeth sharper than the knives I carry. The carnival collapsed on me small as I was a cipher really all I could manage was the cry for Mother the cry that echoes to stone reception. This town has a latitude and a longitude and no one who knows anything goes there. Mars is bigger a healthier salad people fork delight past lips curved shinier than the secrets such pebbles so much grit in my dumb waif shoes. Some other sister who is not mine is driving in on Thursday and there will be a quick galaxy of cake.

The serving is the easy part.

Bad Girls Go To Hell

you hurt people with your words
words are your razors
you tend to say oops
and sorry
until the next nick

you love good sex
which translated means
good for you
you have been orgasmic since twelve
a real accomplishment
considering where you
came from

you know the truth
you spout the truth
you live the truth
lies are for amateurs

you do not care what people think
you do not seek approval
no, not even your mother's
you are not once twice three times a lady
you are considerable reality
much more than the average 21st century male
in pressed khakis and loafers
can contend with

you have danced topless
screamed FUCK YOU at God
and all those pathetic
pretenders to the throne
you have smeared your lipstick
all over grateful cock
talked dirty in respectable married Christian ear
you have loved the men everyone warned you about

you have loved many men
shameless, giddy
sometimes smirking
but always on fire
you have sprinted after love
then changed
your mind

you are a bad girl
and you know where they go
everywhere, darling, everywhere
that's the fucking point.

Daddy Make it Better

He thinks I'm stupid. He thinks I smell bad.
He gives me a book on basic etiquette and a bottle of sex burst perfume.
His new wife is such a fetching bitch.
She has excellent improvisation skills
and a killer ass. I'm sulking in the corner.
The world has treated me like a lesser fish but still I'm gasping
and gutted and frying in butter in some man's skillet while old black
voices croon medicine
on the new moon station.
Some man is going to eat me
with hush puppies
and tartar sauce.
Some man keeps killing me.
I'm living thrash to thrash.
Each day is a deliberate ouch a manic seek
a throaty plunge.
Mother is exasperated.
When is her girl going to start making sense?
The sun. The pond. The rusted toys.
This broiling expanse
so choked with weeds.

Prettier Story

In a prettier version there is no blood on the floor,
no heads on the wall,
no bones stacked sloppy
in the closet.
No one mentions the stench
of burnt witch in the kitchen.
I'm the pale skinny maiden in the tower sitting placid
in the moonlit mirror combing my obedient golden hair.
My eyes are bright flowers
soaking up the rain, not ancient wounds begging
for a physician or shaman, whichever
is handy and awake at four a.m. on a Saturday.
I comb my hair and sing my clarion call,
which you hear and heed on the fastest steed
in the kingdom. You throw your pebbles
at my stained glass window for where I live it is holy
and I am so close to God I can kiss his toes.
The pebbles turn into cupcakes which I eat and because
they are magic and because I am hungry for that sort of thing
the material world melts and I am the spirit behind you holding
onto you with my believing arms and we are riding riding flying flying
and hell does not cannot
bar the way.
I like this version enough to memorize it,
carve it deep into my skin like a favorite book
from childhood with a sea of pages a mermaid with a heart bigger than Alaska
can sing and splash around in.

Sixth Grade is Louder Than it Used To Be

Mr. Bustillos wants to see me after class.
I'll never be an actress. My eyes suggest suicide
and my mouth doesn't open wide enough.
I'm so skinny and mute in the cabin bed I'm invisible as fire ants feast
on my moonsick skin
and the chaperone sleeps a few feet away
dreaming maybe of the next Jesus barbecue.
I don't miss my uterus or those feelings
but they creep between my toes whenever Bon Jovi
assaults my FM radio with his promises
of forever love.
Jon Mark rejected me because my breasts couldn't laugh
and I was pretty much a nonentity, eating lunch alone in the last bathroom stall
until the principal strode across the tile
and told me to come out and join the crowd.
I'm a mother now with breasts bigger than plums
but back then was the only when.
My head is hollow with echoes.

Love When Messy

Love when messy and it always is tells her she is wrong in those feelings so fat
and blatant and forgetful of etiquette
forget morality which never entered
the unframed picture.
He has been wearing the same souvenir t-shirt
three days in a row and also he brags that he
will give her an orgasm like a cat being kicked across
the room and too he shakes the magic 8-ball
and snarls, "Outlook not so good."
Of course there will always be spaghetti sauce drip
and unfresh mouth
and guns that shoot but not very well
and walk of shame dress reeking of
stale smoke
and pussy and beer.
The thing is the tiger the wild the hot the dangerous the lurk
and if you let it then good and if you don't
then boring and it's your funeral, baby, but you don't get to direct it, no,
you don't get to pick
the flowers and the crowd and the venue
and the music.

There Was This Girl

There was this girl this little girl and she was stuck inside a cartoon populated with slobbering wolves, Christian soldiers, used condom salesmen and pseudo chefs. This little girl did not run very fast did not hide very hard she was all lipstick pout bouncy hair nervous giggle squeaky shoes drumbeat heart. Oh! Oh! This girl this girl this very little girl was found and found and found again, tied to trees, tied to tracks, stuck in bubbly stew, shot with arrows, hacked to bits with ambitious ax. She was kissed, too, and the kissing always makes it better. Prayers ascended to God The Saturn like marshmallow smoke and Angel The Venus came down on candy cloud and little girl was saved and saved and saved again, starred in local paper surrounded with inky hearts and breathless witness accounts. This very little girl would never die for good what with so much loopy syndication and cartoons being what they are, sugary dreams you can sleep to and eat to with one eye open while the Chevrolet is warming up.

Libido Will Not Be Televised

Give her the nice Coca-Cola lotion cock and your stopwatch heart for xmas
for valentine's day for national clitoris day just because just because.
Chew him up concise and swallow with sparkling water to show you care.
Keep it clean and concealed inside
a white pastry box.
Smile your bland share your beige at church and the Rotary Club meeting.
Safe inside the monkey house giddy screams
and wild flings are allowed
but hide the cameras from curious fingers
and careful with the belt
and piping hot white cream gravy
can cause blisters to form
and San Francisco will never
be the capital of America.
Meditation on Duluth.
A study in polite contrasts.
Shake the sweaty hand that feeds you raspberry balsamic chicken breasts
and olive oil drizzled asparagus spears.
The magic word is discretion.
A paper shredder is a wise investment.
If she leaves evidence behind
you can burn it
but you cannot
burn her.
Those kind of days
are over.

Trip

In the chill he sleeps loud
beside me in the rented bed
breathing through a mask.
He brought me an orange
and black coffee for breakfast.
His thick fingers dance deft
on my back until I fall
into dreams of terrible snow.
In San Antonio it's late May
and the sun is my mother
screaming birds from the sky.
We park on a hill and look
at the ugly skeletons,
tomorrow's unimaginative mansions.
It's agreed. We both want a garage
and a room for our books.
Sanctuary.
Our smiles are so much older
than photographs suggest.

No Kind of Boat

She was wearing mean mouth
which matched her mean pink bra
because she meant business
and there would be no mistakes.
He watched, distressed, much
less than a monkey, much less a man.
Didn't she like the chicken dinner?
Yes, chicken dinner was fine.
And the wine, a remarkable pinot.
Nothing to pout about, no, no clouds
to piss rain down on hot sex party.
The television cackled the moon
mocked through the blinds and still
there it was
the Atlantic fucking Ocean between them
making him mutter to himself
to his penis
to the remote control
It's Hurricane Season &
I Ain't No Kind Of Boat.

No Romance

He was drunk and I was drunk and I had to convince him and he still wasn't convinced and I told him it was because I wasn't blonde and he told me that was cheap and finally we attempted a kiss but he didn't really want to kiss me he wanted to suck my tongue and it fucking hurt and I sucked his dick but it remained flaccid and I wanted to be fucked and I was fucked but only in my mind which is the worst place and the best place but in this instance it was definitely the worst place and I asked him to go down on me but I was on the rag and he wasn't down with that not in the case of me because I was not blonde and I was cheap and I was married and not to him but he spanked my ass until it was red and I screamed DADDY and later we watched a bunch of rabbits kill people and we laughed at Kris Kross and I bought him a steak and I heard him puke and he stayed with me while I tried to shit and we sat in a bar and he told me about how all the men congregated around the love of his life or one of the loves of his life (a blonde, natch) but there's more to it than hair color he likes his women well-read but sane yet really bubbly and shit and the biggest no no of all was when I got drunk and serenaded him with various crap ass songs the worst being "Hold Me Now" and asked him for a kiss and then got impatient and licked his face and years of friendship were null and void in the ugly whore face of such egregious error and I missed him I loved him for a long fucking time but now I don't and that's the end.

CHOICE

There are choices, honey, there are options.
You can choose to climb out your bedroom window
when you're fourteen years old and fuck your boyfriend and get pregnant,
grow a pet in your uterus then have a cute church wedding
and honeymoon at DisneyWorld
because you are a princess and you are pretty
and he loves you and you know
that can't be bad.
Parents will help out, Christian parents
who believe sex education is evil
and True Love Waits.
Christian parents are really great
at changing diapers and footing bills.
There are choices, there are options.
You can get drunk at a kegger
when you are sixteen years old
and nibble on your boyfriend's ear
and suck his meaty varsity football player cock
and fuck him until the usual stuff spurts out
and does something miraculous to your voluptuous eggs. Grow the miracle
for nine months if you want
then if you think you can hand the miracle over to financially responsible
morally correct
psychologically sound
adoptive parents who know how
to decorate a nursery
and purchase a fully loaded Escalade
and plan Florida vacations
and keep from being killed by bears
at Yellowstone.
There are choices, bitch!
There are options, whore!
You can fuck every willing dick
within a ten mile radius
get knocked up

wonder who manufactured
the miracle
not that it matters
because you are the factory, after all
and you will be the one in stirrups
and you will be probed
and you will be questioned
and you will be accountable
and you and you
(get used to scrutiny)
(sputtering spit)
(pointing fingers)
you fetching bitch
you have all the names.
You make all the lists.
You can go to the zoo
and wish you were a giraffe.
God! If only it were
that fucking easy.
Get the embryo/fetus/sea monkey sucked out
stare up at the cute Garfield poster on the ceiling
get a tattoo so you will never forget
order an extra thick strawberry milkshake
let your mommy mother you
take you shopping for sexy but not slutty shoes
get your fingernails and toenails painted Silly Tulip
call your boyfriend
invite him to the hot shit homecoming dance.
Don't tell anyone about it.
This is your secret.
Hide the bump with an ironic Mrs. Roper housecoat
those are always in style
push that sucker out behind Taco Cabana
throw the brat in the dumpster
wash your hands
eat some nachos

soothe yourself with soda
and big fucking plans.
There are sales down the street.
Someday you will know more shit
and shit will be easier
and you will be in control
and it's your body
and this is your world
and maybe you'll be a brain surgeon
and maybe you'll be President of the United States
and maybe you'll be the one to pioneer Mars
but right now
there are colors to code
facts to file
and which dress tonight
and which earrings
and which dick
and everything sucks
but it's fun to pretend
like that
is not
the case.

Texan American Fairy Tale

Okay, he says. The hot dog casserole is in the oven.
I put broccoli in it. It should be good.

I've ruined the pine table with acrylic paint splatter.
I've made the ugly carpet uglier with hair dye stains.
I'm 25K in student loan debt and I cannot hold down an American
entry level job. In 2006 I was a security guard for a few months
until he gave me permission to stay home and write while he fielded
phone calls from irate T-Mobile customers. Assholes.
God! I wish the biggest problem on my plate was a fucking cell
phone bill.
He sold his car so we could make the poetry gig
in Las Vegas because my name, my beautiful
six syllable name, was on the bright yellow flyer.
He wrote a book about our three days in Las Vegas
and published it himself and sent copies
to our friends.

We'll love each other again in San Antonio, he says.
We'll be tender. We'll bring the magic back.
We deserve a house. We deserve barbecues,
trips to California, trips to Ireland and Germany...
our son deserves this, a mommy and daddy
who love each other and fill photo albums
with ebullient proof
of the American dream, grasped.

I dream of a cabin in Oregon, a studio apartment
in San Francisco, a flimsy shelter made of palm fronds on some
unnamed island
in the South Pacific.
My heart is the kind of dog that does not stay.
I stay but I'm gone.
I'm not a wife but a cipher.
He loves me.

I stay.

In McKinney, Texas where mansions manufactured
by the ghost of Walt Disney stick their tongues out
and sing song What War? What Depression?
Ain't We Got FUN?!
we sit across from each other in a Tex-Mex restaurant eating chicken
flautas talking like our tongues have not turned black
from so much effort, so much loss.
He doesn't see what I see.
I'm watching the suspended television behind his head. Nazis are shoving
naked Jews into a ditch.
Won't the Holocaust ever fucking end?

This world is not acceptable.
I reject the whole thing.
But today I am driving home in a hail damaged SUV because he got a loan
and the color, black cherry,
is more poetic than beige.
Buddy Holly sings his yearning on the stereo
and I smile the cynical twist of a ravaged crone.
I don't know
how I
got here.

I Woke Up My Heart

I woke up my heart in a panic reaching for the radio or a bottle of whiskey my socks sweaty with disco my compass in my stomach accidental swallow ants chasing crumbs down my bad woman legs spread wider than Australia the coach a rotting pumpkin again the men all rats fighting for my cherry center strobe lit throb darling of the dance darling I'm afraid my card has been filled chewed pissed on burned at bad girl stake there are no leftovers here you cannot eat bone but meanwhile in the closet heels and dresses gather for next celebration my heart my heart coming back to life!

This One He Reads

This is the love letter he reads and reads again
uncomfortable in his blistering chair.
The bridge burned, the map erased,
there's nothing for it
not even a backward glance.
Smoke gets in your eyes and you turn
to salt or stone.
There is only this, the love letter he reads
and reads again
commits to memory inside his box
made of steel.
Lions roared higher than mountains
and roses raged with sea.
Promises were pentacles sharp and black.
Somehow a trespass, a breaking through
and clouds rolling past pretending
not to notice.
Cups spilled rubies and rainbows
and we were lucky inside that space.
There were rings on my toes and magic in my hair
and when I looked at you I saw you
and seeing you
you saw me
and we knew
we knew with all our might
and we danced as if we were sixteen
tremendous with blazing light
the monster night could devour whatever it wanted
but not us
but not us.
That was the song
and it carried us laughing
into heaven.
I'm bleeding with stained glass

but this is common
and happening all over the planet
as trees sigh their wisdom
and birds busy with chirp
do not listen.
The love was such a buzz
such a decadent consume
it happened so fast and furious
he could not feel it.
He is feeling it now.
This is the last letter, the one he reads
the one he keeps
deep inside his ice
his fingers sadder
than unmarked paper.

Desperate Promotion

Come here now come see come watch
lovesick mother you would like to fuck
taking it all off with practiced smirk
sucking on a lollipop like Lolita
buzzing vibrating bunny ears
against luscious nectarine clit.
Tits. Ass. Tits. Ass. Tits. Ass.
Free brazen display expressly for you.
Cubicle work is such a grind.
It helps the corporate drone mind to focus
on something fresh and unexpected.
Pussy direct to your inbox.
Look at those long legs spread so wide for you
welcoming you into hot sex world
so fucking sultry so insanely shameless
you can smell that carnivorous cunt
from a thousand miles away.
Cheerleader. Nurse. Catholic schoolgirl.
Exotic dancer. Mistress. Whore.
Naughty Valentine
a few years late.

Fucking Ugly Discounted Bitch

I give good love, friendship on fire,
and then I get shit on and spit on
and the pretty melts and the angelic mutates
and then
and then.

I am not any man's amazing dream come true.
I don't boil bunnies or wield a butcher knife.
I'm too much of a pussy.
I hide in my little bitch cave and dance
my dangerous witch cunt fingers across
the black keyboard.
I tell what needs to be told because no fury in hell
matches the fury of an untouched clitoris.
Of course I can give myself all the love I need.
Of course that is the biggest lie of all.
I wanted to be remembered.
I made damn sure that I would be.

How Deep My Ugly

Stick a toe in. You never felt so much cold ink.
This tacky freak show writes itself.
Smiling vagina refrigerated absence of something civil like grape jelly, maybe,
or chocolate milk.
Tits and ass giddy with reveal. April sparkles all over November.
The starry distance makes it okay.
How deep my ugly and wide my desperate and high my hunger and
so many mouths below confused with eyes and the carnival
is me stuck puking at the top.
Once I was ten and fine on my bike and Daddy was gone and Mom
was at work and I was ten and fine on my bike riding to the arcade
with Jeff who gave me tokens so that I would leave him alone.
The babysitters loved me. I was so wild, no telling what I would toss
out the window next.
The cousin spiked my Coke with salt.
I danced myself into an asthma attack.
Daddy was gone and I was hungry and there was no carpet and there
was a pervert who asked to see your panties in the laundromat but I
was armed with Windex and Southern Baptist angels protected
my virginity.
I would grow up and marry Shane or
someone similar.
The slutty little blonde bitch showed Shane
her pink panties and I was scared he would
like her more than he could like me
because I didn't go around doing that sort of thing
but he walked out of the house holding my hand
and no one
has ever
loved me more than that.

Spoiled

It is spoiled now, ruined, but he gives me the last cheeseburger and lets me stay.
A bitch strays but always comes home and begs, wagging that tail, making those
noises that can only mean Love Me Please Although I Don't Deserve It.

When the oven doesn't fit there is this and the poison leaks
and we all drink it and die
so slow
it feels like swimming
in a Texas lake
when the fireworks have fizzled
and the trucks
have gone home.

FUCK DOLL

I'll have the usual, he says.

His voice is lazy.

His voice doesn't have to try very hard.

Finger crook. Wink. Nudge. Dollar bill.

White teeth flash. Predator dazzle.

Killer charisma.

Kill me and get it over with, she says.

Fuck dolls do not have a voice.

Fuck dolls are forever on the menu.

Letters made of blood. Menstrual jelly on buttery toast.

Die for any kind of connection. This is cheap. This will serve.

He tells her she smells like coconuts. She is nice. She is flexible.

She does the dance.

Your breasts are perfect, he says.

Perfection is something to strive for.

You taste good. That is the assurance. There was doubt.

Affirm. Appease. It's a kind of dance. Toes bruised with tango.

He comes down from ego mountain to fake a grovel to play at squirm.

Pussy manna. Man the pussy is thick tonight. Pussy soup. Pussy saves.

Fuck doll deflates. Fuck doll is stored in bulging closet.

It's a kind of tacky little buffet. It's a kind of beggar's ball.

All the lights shine red with GO.

Green is the wrong color. Green suggests depth and magic and linger.

The finger is on the red button and everything pulses.

Pass the sugar, darling. We are fat with whimsy.

Singular Cry

The drumsticks will be ready soon. What are drumsticks? I think they're chicken legs. Yes. That's what they are. The chicken legs will be ready soon. A package of several chicken legs was purchased at a grocery store this morning. The grocery store is located in Corsicana, Texas. The chicken legs were seasoned with garlic salt and black pepper then placed inside a hot oven. Right now the chicken legs are baking but not burning. They should be ready soon.

Sometimes the lights go out. It's sudden and unexpected whenever the lights go out. The baby is scared but the mother knows the darkness isn't anything to be afraid of. The mother lights two little candles. One candle is vanilla scented. The other candle is blue and its scent is difficult to define. It isn't blueberry. It isn't freesia. It isn't baby butt powder. The candles are never lit. Whenever the lights go out the candles are lit. The lights do not usually go out.

There are bottles of wine and champagne in the refrigerator. No one here is an alcoholic. People here drink milk, water, juice and ginger ale. The ginger ale is not cold. The ginger ale is not located inside the refrigerator. The ginger ale is in a plastic bottle. The plastic bottle is located on the counter. There are pills on the counter but no one takes those. It's quiet here. You can hear the hum of things.

Once there was a carnival down the road. It was night and the carnival boasted loud lights and popular music. People rode rides and won prizes. People ate popcorn, jumbo pretzels, cotton candy, pickles, nachos, corn dogs, hot dogs and funnel cakes. Shoes got dirty. Children screamed. Teenagers kissed and groped. In another field near the high school there were hot air balloons. The hot air balloons did not ascend very high. There wasn't anywhere to go but up, up above telephone wires and houses and churches and banks and the grocery store and the gas station and the post office and the park.

Sometimes in Texas at least in 1984 the mothers fed their

children biscuits for breakfast. The biscuits were hot from the oven. To make the biscuits taste better butter was added and grape jelly or maple syrup. Texas mothers sometimes fed Texas children biscuits for breakfast with orange juice to drink. This was common in 1984. Another breakfast possibility at least in Texas in 1984 was Malt-O-Meal with butter and sugar. There was also cinnamon toast to consider. Strawberries were never for breakfast. Blueberries were never for breakfast. Bananas were never for breakfast. Fried pork chops were sometimes served for breakfast in Texas in 1984. No one knew what granola was. No one knew about yogurt.

When a girl is pretty it's easy. A pretty girl can smile and lisp and wear the right clothes. A pretty girl can hang out at the mall with her friends. This happens often in America. Pretty girls hang out in food courts with their pretty friends. They shop for shoes and bracelets and body lotion, which is available in numerous exciting scents. Life in America is easy for pretty girls who giggle and shop and know how to Facebook and Twitter. The path is wide for pretty American girls. The future opens wide for pretty American girls who wear the right clothes and go to the right parties. There are limitless choices. Pretty American girls can go to law school. They can stay right where they are and get married to popular football players. The popular football players work for their wealthy grandfathers and buy houses and cars and diamonds for pretty American girls. The American calendar is fat for reasons to celebrate, at least for pretty American girls. A pretty American girl will never be homeless or hopeless. She can be a fashion model. She can be an actress. She can be a whore. She can be an exotic dancer. She can be a kept woman, which is common in 2012 America. The pretty girls who become pretty women are kept in pretty houses. There are walls to decorate. Pinterest helps pretty American women figure out what to put on all those pretty blank walls.

If you are insane and live in rural Texas you will not have any friends. No one will give a good goddamn if you live or die. You can piss and moan about it, write books about it, scrawl I WAS HERE in bathroom stalls but no one will believe you no one will feel you no one will know you. No. You will not be known. There are all kinds of tragedies in the world. This is only one.

Demon Owl

The owl is so fucking insistent.
Hooting its goddamn ass off
like it has so much wisdom to impart.
What are you trying to tell me, owl?
Are you asking me to explain myself?
I don't have to but I will.
I don't owe you my revelations.
Here they are.
I am the lady who lived beyond the fire.
I got done in God's oven.
No mouth will gnaw me now.
No man will know me.
I'm angel witch of peculiar dawn.
I sit here in ashes spinning webs.
Make a record, it lasts longer.

Missing Baby

The baby was lost the baby could not be found for all the cigarette butts, crack pipes, wine bottles, easy listening records, barely legal magazines, fetish boutique receipts and fast food garbage. Dead rats and dead cockroaches added that something extra to the earth tone living room. All the walls were painted Desert Throb. There was a baby but the baby was missing and was not crying so the baby was impossible to find. Of course the television was yammering its butt cream commercials and rollicking good time sitcoms, same as always. Henrietta was dreaming of deflated cocks on the couch. Avery was inside a box of some kind, punishing himself. A knock on the door meant the Christian volunteer had exciting news to spread.

Disregard

Nothing was put into perspective during the $2 show at the planetarium. The universe still swallows me I am still a cipher and I still believe I'm cursed with an Aquarius sun and Virgo moon and my Mercury in Pisces explains the whole goddamn thing, the nubby fabric of my lackluster life. The show was more didactic than transcendent, a balding scientist with a droll delivery explaining to tiny brain me that it would take aliens too long to reach our planet and why would they bother and astrology is one more myth to debunk and bury behind grandpappy's barn and anyone who doubts we put a man on the moon is an idiot drooling in her Lucky Charms. I've sent e-mail I should not have sent burnt bridges that never should have been built eaten soggy Dairy Queen nachos and sent my son off to play with his imaginary siblings while I tap my fingers like this dance means something like it gets me somewhere like I'm not standing in one place dizzy inside the celestial zoom that does not calculate the mosquito buzz of my damaged neurons. My back aches and I want to sleep and dream of nothing. I want to be buried in snow. Things will start making sense inside that cold blank my frosty nothing death. There were dinosaurs there are things that live in the darkest part of the ocean despite the boiling heat there are wasps waiting for me in the laundry room there are cardboard boxes filled with toys and books and cheap winter clothes and receipts and plastic cards and plastic spoons and plastic forks and nobody loves me everybody hates me but the birds have eaten all of the worms. Germany is further away than Pluto. California is closer than my bright pink vibrator. I live and breathe California even though I have never surfed or sold any books at Beyond Baroque or read my poems at Bird and Beckett. I'm a bag lady in training I carry several lifetimes around and suck at small talk and social pleasantries unless I am talking to myself. I save ketchup packets and birthday candles because you never fucking know. I've got a lot of pennies. I've got too many books. I paint I write I wonder when the world will be done with me, finally. What else is required? Do I have to show up? My back is aching. I don't want to be here. I don't want this dance. I don't want these words. Fly away, birds, you will never be hawks or eagles or even buzzards. I have no power I have no voice I have no choice I have no salve no solution no sunny days with smiling friends who favor me with pet names and piggyback rides. I've done the bride thing the daughter thing the sister thing the mother thing the whore thing the Valentine returned to sender thing and I am not winging a goddamn thing I'm limping down the road with my eyes on the dirt. Red rover red rover I couldn't break through so I'm here with you until the machine shuts down and God the bell rings me home. God I anticipate that clarion call. I've been an angel all along. I've done my time with the crickets and the dogs and the drunk cheerleaders. I've worn the freak flag to shreds and never asked for a threaded needle. There's a hole for me a sanctuary a final rest a castle made of mud. I'm trudging toting my weary load of gladdest rags. There are ravaged hags happier than I will ever be. The jukebox plays all the wrong songs and what I want is not on the menu and there will be no more kisses no moony missing across puke splattered miles. The map is a stone inside my gut. I can show you how to get there. My sleeping son is the only beautiful thing the only valuable truth and I know I will lose him like I lose everything else. I don't hold gold it slips through my fingers. This has all been my fault my shoddy production there is no one else to blame. I'm through with life but life is not through with me. My back aches and I don't want to be sitting here doing this dance telling everything that has already been told. The eyes have seen my glory my gory my story in bold screaming black ALL CAPS. I'm the fool in the corner. Disregard.

Daily Bread

I'm fat in my purple shower cap and leopard print gown drinking hot coffee from a California mug. I'm such a cliche, a middle-aged woman who gave too much to love and sits on her ass staring forty in the face, wretched with self-loathing and regret. I should not have flashed those tits. I should not have sucked that dick. I should have saved all those Snoopy stamps, slaved over a hot typewriter instead of a stove. Wait. I am Snoopy. I have opened my veins and bled on a lifetime of blank pages. I have followed my bark to the rainbow with blinders on, left the xmas tree to Charlie Brown and his lisping pals. I have been alone with myself. In matters of the heart I have not had dry spells. I've had the fucking Gobi. So why am I here now wishing I had run away with the circus. The circus ran away with me. That's me on the trapeze. That's me splattered amongst an infinity of peanut shells. That's me drowning in elephant piss. That's me the psychotic unicycling clown crying in my cotton candy. I have run I have sprinted I have bled I have given unto death and half-hearted applause. Here I am now black coffee bitter and bitching about my missing slice of American Pie. When you're on disability for insanity you tend to doubt your role in the grand scheme of things, tend to look up at the sky and envy the clouds and the goddamn birds. I envy balloons, the ones filled with helium, the ones that leave my son's fingers and float above the trees and disappear. I would like to disappear but that would be rather rude of me. That would solve nothing. I'm sick of my slobber, sick of my hollow, sick of my ungodly hunger, my unholy strive. What the fuck what the suck what the truck what the buck am I trying for? What is there at the end of this sentence? I am not in prison. I am not Hansel in the cage behind the candy house. I am free to dig wishing wells, feed the swans, collect the rampion, catch the white stag, run my freak flag up the pole and see for miles. Seeing for miles has burned the blue from my eyes. I don't want to see. I don't want to hear. I don't want to touch. I don't want to feel. I'm back to Rapunzel envy. Give me a tower made of stones with one high window. Put a song in my throat but don't let a prince ride by on a horse made of cream and sugar no don't let a horny prince happen to hear all the shit

I got to say. I don't ache for rescue. That never works. I ache for the knife and the stone the quill and the page but I have that I've got that and I am still here in my purple shower cap and leopard print gown not sexy at all in my flip-flops not relevant not heavy light as a feather and in the breeze and not wanted not caught not needed not grasped. I'm sending postcards from hell but there is not enough postage and the recipients are lost at sea. I need to buy bread. I need to buy pillows. I need to buy a comb for all these tangles. Oh song my mouth. So strong my south. And long and long and forever my route. I'm about to die if I cannot live higher and better and prettier than this. I'm the crone turned to stone the lone warrior crusty with blood in the forgotten woods. Praise me for my presence, goddamn it. I'm here I'm alive every fucking day is my birthday a miracle of candles and cake and purple and green streamers. I'm not a celebrity. I'm not an American success to story. I'm rags to rags. I'm a scarecrow. Stuffed. Stuck. I can't come down. Oh god oh fuck oh shit oh piss oh hell oh damn I'm tired of not breathing not walking beneath the moon and Jupiter with tingling skin and aching feet. I need a new kind of ache. I need a new kind of weary. I need to burn to sweat to be alive and at home in my body. These demons have dragged me down into an idiot sea and they aren't done with me yet but I am done with them. I'm soaring. I'm out of it. I'm telling you...I'm gone.

Dishes

She was washing dishes her hands were pink and raw and artificial lemon scented and flies were buzzing around and he did not notice he was on the loveseat in the den watching "The Bachelor." Her stomach was filled with bell pepper and mushroom pizza and pinot grigio and she loathed herself because she wanted to lose thirty pounds had wanted to lose thirty pounds for fifteen years but wasn't doing anything about it wasn't drinking ten glasses of water a day eating hard-boiled eggs for breakfast and tuna fish and asparagus for lunch and boneless skinless chicken breasts seasoned with sea salt and black pepper for dinner wasn't doing yoga wasn't running three miles three times a week wasn't power walking laps inside a mall wasn't drinking black coffee wasn't drinking green tea wasn't snorting speed. There were no children there were no cats there were no dogs there were no hamsters there were no fish there were no sea monkeys. "It's a jungle out there," she said. The kitchen window was black because it was night outside the window and there were no lights and the moon was a puny crescent but he never mowed the backyard so she knew from memory it was indeed a jungle out there a jungle made not of trees and monkeys and snakes and panthers but of weeds and bugs and feral cats. The backyard was a jungle but she was speaking also of the world itself the world of rural Texas which was quiet enough except for the occasional drunk antagonistic redneck and except for the yapping of the redneck dogs and the mewling of the feral cats in heat and the incessant buzzing of the crickets and the whine of the train going wherever it went. It was rural Texas it was quiet nothing happened there was no crime there was no traffic people walked to the convenience store to buy Funyuns and beer and beef jerky and cigarettes and lottery cards. She did not mean jungle in the usual sense of the word she did not mean a jungle of rape and theft and burglary and hijacking and rival gangs pissing on their turf slashing throats with Mexican knives blowing heads off with Russian revolvers she meant jungle in the sense of what a fucking waste of humanity people pissing and moaning from cradle to grave scratching heads and asses farting apathetic ugly and mediocre in comfort zone of mindless sitcoms and reality television and car wrecks and pageant winners on the news and sorry Fourth of July fireworks displays at the lake and too much light beer and too much Jesus and too much family and not enough space not enough true wild not enough mountain climb river swim desert crawl Walden Ed Abbey what the fuck ever testing some kind of personal limit going for some kind of spiritual intangible gold keeping the gold sacred holding it deep inside not giving it away not letting it spill keeping the fire burning bright marking boundaries telling nosy ass bitches and cocksuckers this is mine do not touch do not trespass this is my air to breathe my starscape to traverse you are not allowed you do not know the secret code. She dried off her hands on a faded orange dish towel the dishes were done the dishes were clean and dry and put away she went outside to the car port which was dark lit a cigarette a menthol cigarette looked into the blackness the black jungle that was the backyard thought about nothing inhaled frosty smoke exhaled liked the taste in her mouth closed her eyes saw nothing felt nothing she was married she had a husband he was inside sitting on the loveseat in the den watching a rich white man court skinny white women in Switzerland and Costa Rica later they would share a bed and there would be no sex and he would snore and she would read a book of essays written by rich white women who had sucked a few cocks and won a few awards and spent time in a few big deal cities such as Manhattan and San Francisco and Seattle and Vancouver and Berlin and Milan and Paris and London they knew a few things she did not know maybe they were married or had been married but they had gone they had seen they had really fucking felt and really fucking lived. She smoked five more cigarettes then went back inside the house and drank another glass of pinot grigio then she brushed her teeth and washed her face then took off her clothes put on a Betty Boop gown and got in bed.

Please Don't Google My Name

I was little and didn't know anything so They told me stuff.
Mostly They told me about Three being One.
There is a God, he's the biggest, he's the Daddy of them all.
There is a son, he's Jesus, a necessary pawn.
There is a ghost called Holy Spirit that will come into your heart.
You need the Three. You need the One. So much love in one package.

I had nightmares about the Rapture, the Tribulation, the Bottomless Pit.
When I was nine my mother took me to the funeral home to see my cousin.
I did not want to see his dead body in the coffin but I saw it.
He became the star of my apocalyptic dreams.
He was in the pit trying to crawl out.
I was of no use.

The most terrifying thing was the account, The Movie.
When you die God shows you a movie of your life.
I know this because They told me so.
I had to live through so many things once.
I did not want to have to live through it all again when dead,
sharing popcorn and Milk Duds with God and his angels.
So I stopped believing Them, in pieces.
I threw a lot of dolls and books out of a lot of windows.
There have been a few bonfires.

Today the universe is banging down my door.
"Mothers, be careful what you say to your children. Your words become their inner voice."
My son is sick, it might be strep throat.
Yesterday I drove the car with the broken air conditioner
all over Leon Valley looking for Sonic,
my son sweating in his carseat
wearing the Black Panther mask
his father made out of construction paper.
I screamed curses at San Antonio, at Leon Valley, at Texas,

at the goddamn sun.
My son cried and said he loved San Antonio
because of the Tower of The Americas.
He wanted cheese sticks and a Sprite.
I found Sonic and paid for his snack with quarters
taken from his robot bank.
The father calls me from the clinic, asks me where
our son was born, how much he weighed, if I
took medication during my pregnancy.
My son is sick, it might be strep throat.
There are Popsicles in the freezer.
I think I might be a robot.
I keep bumping into brick walls.
Words are losing all meaning.
I'm sick, it might be a lifelong affliction.
Up until five a.m. Googling Hollie Stevens,
finding much light, much horror.
Hollie Stevens transcended the shit ass carnival.
I think I might be wallowing in it.
I think I might need new batteries.

I fly away to be a mermaid
then come home to Texas
where I am reminded with each piece of bread, each drop of wine,
that I'm ugly and broken and not fooling anyone.
Words are losing all meaning.
My inner voice is no kind of map.
I'm driving around Texas looking for a place to park.
My son's voice is behind me
asking me why some of the flags are flying
from the top of the poles
and some of the flags are stuck
in the middle.
He wanted to see the latest Stan Lee extravaganza.
He wanted to wear 3D glasses.
I took him I took it I sat there and cringed.

I never fought in Vietnam
so why the fuck am I so goddamn shell-shocked?

I've thrown a lot of dolls and books from a lot of windows.
I can't count all the bonfires.

Sometime This Spring

Everything wills it.
I will step out of this box
like I'm going for a drink of water.
The heavy clothes will puddle at my feet.
The fresh air will burn my lungs
the blazing blue sky will deafen me
the waiting earth will welcome me
with a mother mouth, deep and ravaged mother heart
accepting the sorry gift of me
as if I were made
of shinier stuff.

Exact Recitations

Puzzle strong in my bower no pentacles could purchase
no swords could fell my wintry edifice with the secret
code no fists could knock. His spider messenger
guessed my nickname (appendage) so I gave him
the faith of nightfall, slipped out of my solitude
which was an ill-fitting hand-me-down crumble
from Cherokee grandmother's cedar scented trousseau.
"Is that a full house in your hands or are you-"
"My darling I could not be more glad to see you."
"What am I now? A major reward?"
"You're the lamp in the window. Let 'em watch you shine."

He swooped me up because I was strong black coffee
and he was rakish in his wide awake eyes and the grocer
had the eggs ready for us on the shelf, not broken, not expired
in a silly goose gleaming fragile dreaming row.

(in the wings those ever present cackles, fat & white with delight)

Uncle Remus is Not Racist

I could be a better mother. This song has been ringing in my ears for four and a half years while trains and clouds make me sick with envy. I'm trying to love yogurt and Goethe and Sonic Youth, hate Chef Boyardee pizza and Sylvia Plath and Gary Stewart. My son hands me his beautifully illustrated Jack in The Beanstalk and I read the voices in a Cockney accent. His big blue eyes widen and he sucks his thumb with nervous fury when I become the giant ogre hungry for boy blood. My hair is crazy…too long too black too thick too curly. When I pick my son up from preschool a little girl tells her friends, "She looks like a witch." I am a witch, yes, like Yoko Ono, but I am not magic enough to snag an exhibition and a soul mate who takes his mommy anger out on a Rickenbacker. I cannot count all the crushes and affairs on two hands but the last one was enough to turn me off dick for at least a couple of years even though I never met the guy or his dick. It was all virtual, as so many things are. These ugly voices come to me from the rotten woodwork. Fucking cockroaches. Why Are You So Hard On Your Dolls? You're Supposed To Be Tough, Cool And Hip So Act Like It. You Are Insane. Fancy Yourself A Model, Eh? My son should know how to write his name by now. Thanks to his grandmother he knows that Jesus and Santa Claus are always watching him. I don't watch him enough. I go inside my room, turn off the light, close the door, get in bed and wish on the glow in the dark stars affixed to the ceiling above my bed. I'm still six but some days I am twelve and jonesing for a bike and a boyfriend who will ride roller coasters with me and win me a purple unicorn. All I can do is show my son the Tar Baby clip and tell him that Uncle Remus is not racist and Huckleberry Finn is a good book and there is a magical place called New Orleans where Mommy realized her destiny on Bourbon Street when she was in first grade. He scribbles tornadoes in his spiral notebook and says, "Lucky people can drive during a tornado." I tell him, "Yes, baby, but lucky people are not us. We can never drive during a tornado. When the siren sounds we have to hide in the tub beneath a blanket. It's not up to us to defy the sky."

Soaked With Love

Technical about it
a sticky girl
who should not did.
Who looks stupid now?
Bloody fish and this
is not the way to go.
His hand so able cannot undo.
Dirty with Texas
diamonds lose shine.
Dead with monotonous
killer high heels.
Bar jokes showing
it ends up in ditches
even sadder than
the same Charlie Rich song
thick with stuck.

Trash Orange

Once it happens it is over but it can be repeated. Nothing is louder
than organic pears and smiling white bread jesus bromides in my face
except for stuck sister pebbles at my window.
The pool is pink with dead and fallen things.
Those are not unicorn stars in your soup which is why I hide
in closets from census drones and sleep through assembly.
I am fifteen and ghostish my blood so rosy on slumber party sheets.
The roaring train the cyclone the boardwalk coaster
the clattering bag lady cart stuffed with styrofoam
my mermaid detritus
my patchwork quilt
of thick clean nights.

Ramona's Monologue

The woman is sitting on a bed in a cheap motel room in Galveston, Texas. Maybe she's wearing a cheap leopard print gown. Maybe she's wearing Dopey (The Disney dwarf) pajama pants and a Jimi Hendrix t-shirt. She's definitely talking on the phone. Not the cell phone. The cheap motel room standard issue beige phone with a curly cord. She's definitely drinking Jack Daniels (not Jim Beam! not Maker's Mark!) from the bottle. She's definitely smoking a menthol cigarette. Probably a Kool. Religious icon candles are lit. The television is not turned on. The television, in fact, has been thrown out the window, Keith Moon style.

Your fucking machine. I'm always getting your fucking machine. Goddamn it, I said I wouldn't call again and humiliate myself further. But I'm drunk. You know how I get. I came to the ocean to escape and what do I see...yeah, couples all over the motherfucking beach. Smug ass motherfuckers holding hands. Kissing. Fucking. I haven't actually seen any fucking but I know it's there. They're so delirious drunk off their asses on kisses and cum. I can see the cum in their eyes. That doesn't sound right. Sounds like a dirty joke. I had this epiphany a couple of hours ago in the shower. I was drunk then. I'm drunker now. I told myself because there was no one else to tell. Men can be deeply in love with a woman even if the sex is bad. But a woman cannot be deeply in love with a man if the sex is bad. That isn't the truth, though. The sex was always bad with you. Shit, we never even had sex. We had psycho erotic chutes & ladders. I'd advance a few spaces, climb up a lucky ladder, then slide down the chute into a vat of monkey soup. You know what the fuck I'm talkin' about, darlin'. That's why I love you. We spoke the same language. I never had to hand you Cliff's Notes or cue cards. There have been men. Boys. Mannequins. With me sitting beside them on the futon bored out of my fucking skull. We were together but we weren't. It was an orange juice commercial. It was a badly scripted Lifetime movie with me in a bad wig and a worse dress, cum stained, showing off my groveling blow job bruises. The lesson to learn, the truth that buzzes in my blood like a wasp I can never kill, is don't be with someone just to be with someone. If you can't sit beside another human being in the blue television glow and feel like you're being brain fucked on Jupiter, what's the fucking point? Popcorn isn't that lonely. Not even when it's Cracker Jacks with a shit ass prize. There were so many prizes with you. That last morning when you hugged me then walked away I walked around that park in San Francisco with all the huge painted hearts. I was wearing my pajamas. I couldn't stop crying. I wanted to die there. But I didn't die. I got on the plane back to Texas and wrote a book about you. There have been men there have been boys there have been Bee Gees songs and cheap Valentines crusty with cum. Game shows. Strip mall mockery. In the middle of it all me standing still, stuck on rewind, dazed and stupid inside a Bob Dylan song. That Sam Cooke song. "A Change is Gonna Come." I never heard that song until you told me about that bar in New Orleans where you would play that song on the jukebox. I've been listening to that song on YouTube ever since. You're the big fat thing I can't grapple to the ground and destroy. I can't bury you. God, how I want to. But you're the meat. You're the knife. You're the gun pointed at my malfunctioning brain. I said I wouldn't call again but I'm taking orders from the moon and the ocean. I'm five years old and camped out in your backyard. It's 1975 and I'm wearing rainbow disco socks and you're licking fondue from your fingers. Not chocolate fondue. No, baby, you're licking that cheese fondue and mocking me with Elvis lyrics. I'm going to not sleep now. I'm going to hang up and listen to the ocean. It's singing our song.

www.ingramcontent.com/pod-product-compliance
Lightning Source LLC
Chambersburg PA
CBHW021123080526
44587CB00010B/612